SERIAL MURDERERS

SERIAL MURDERERS

JAMES T. LAWSON
EDITOR

Nova Science Publishers, Inc.
New York

For permission to use material from this book please contact us:
Telephone 631-231-7269; Fax 631-231-8175
Web Site: http://www.novapublishers.com

LIBRARY OF CONGRESS CATALOGING-IN-PUBLICATION DATA

ISBN: 978-1-60692-204-0

Published by Nova Science Publishers, Inc. ; New York

CONTENTS

PREFACE

The topic of serial murder occupies a unique niche within the criminal justice community. In addition to the significant investigative challenges they bring to law enforcement, serial murder cases attract an over-abundance of attention from the media, mental health experts, academia, and the general public. While there has been significant, independent work conducted by a variety of experts to identify and analyze the many issues related to serial murder, there have been few efforts to reach a consensus between law enforcement and other experts, regarding these matters.

This book is based on information from who have successfully investigated and apprehended serial killers; mental health, academic, and other experts who have studied serial killers and shared their expertise through education and publication; officers of the court, who have judged, prosecuted, and defended serial killers; and members of the media, who inform and educate the public when serial killers strike. A variety of topics covered are related to serial murder including common myths, definitions, typologies, pathology and causality, forensics, the role of the media, prosecution issues, investigative task force organization, and major case management issues.

This book is a culmination of the input and discussion on the major issues related to serial murder. The goal in publishing this book is to outline the consensus views from a variety of disciplines on the causality, motivations, and characteristics of serial murderers, which will enable the criminal justice community to generate a more effective response in the identification, investigation, and adjudication of these cases.

In: Serial Murderers
Editor: James T. Lawson, pp. 1
ISBN: 978-1-60692-204-0

MESSAGE FROM DIRECTOR MUELLER

Every day, law enforcement offi cers across America are called to respond to murders. Each homicide case is tragic, but there are few cases more heartrending and more diffi cult to understand than serial murder.

For years, law enforcement investigators, academics, mental health experts, and the media have studied serial murder, from Jack the Ripper in the late 1800s to the sniper killings in 2002, and from the "Zodiac Killer" in California to the "BTK Killer" in Kansas. These diverse groups have long attempted to understand the complex issues related to serial murder investigations. Until the Serial Murder Symposium, however, there had been few attempts to reach a consensus on some of these issues. This monograph presents the fi ndings and collective wisdom of a multidisciplinary group of experts, who brought their individual experience and insights to the same table. Our hope is that it will give you new ideas and new resources as you continue your important work. The FBI is committed to contributing to the understanding of these horrifi c acts. The FBI's National Center for the Analysis of Violent Crime stands ready to assist our state, local, and international partners. We believe the best way to combat any threat — be it terrorism, gang violence, or serial murder — is to combine our knowledge and resources with those of our partners, and to work as a team. I am grateful for the partnerships that helped spur this symposium, and for the partnerships that were formed as a result. I deeply appreciate the work that went into this publication. I would like to thank all those who participated for their willingness to share their dedication, time and expertise. I believe it will be invaluable to our collective ability to understand, respond to, and hopefully prevent, serial murder

Robert S. Mueller, III

In: Serial Murderers
Editor: James T. Lawson, pp. 3
ISBN: 978-1-60692-204-0

ACKNOWLEDGMENTS

The NCAVC would like to gratefully acknowledge the contributions of the following individuals, without whose efforts the Symposium and this monograph would not have been possible:

The members of the Serial Murder Symposium Working Group, for their assistance in planning the Symposium. The names of these individuals are listed in Appendix B.

The Symposium attendees, for their generous sharing of time and expertise in the area of serial murder. The names of these individuals are listed in Appendix C.

Pamela Hairfield and Wilma Wulchak, Management and Program Analysts, FBI, NCAVC, for their skill, dedication, and perseverance in successfully handling the countless administrative tasks associated with the Symposium.

Cristie Dobson, Management and Program Assistant, FBI, NCAVC, for her talent and time spent copyediting this document and for her work on the cover art.

Assistant Director Michael J. Wolf (retired) and Executive Assistant Director J. Stephen Tidwell for their support of this project and for their willingness to dedicate the resources necessary for its successful completion.

In: Serial Murderers
Editor: James T. Lawson, pp. 5-6
ISBN: 978-1-60692-204-0

FOREWORD

The topic of serial murder occupies a unique niche within the criminal justice community. In addition to the significant investigative challenges they bring to law enforcement, serial murder cases attract an over-abundance of attention from the media, mental health experts, academia, and the general public. While there has been signifi cant, independent work conducted by a variety of experts to identify and analyze the many issues related to serial murder, there have been few efforts to reach a consensus between law enforcement and other experts, regarding these matters.

In an effort to bridge the gap between the many views of issues related to serial murder, the Federal Bureau of Investigation (FBI) hosted a multi-disciplinary Symposium in San Antonio, Texas, on August 29, 2005 through September 2, 2005. The goal of the Symposium was to bring together a group of respected experts on serial murder from a variety of fields and specialties, to identify the commonalities of knowledge regarding serial murder.

A total of 135 subject matter experts attended the five-day event. These individuals included law enforcement officials who have successfully investigated and apprehended serial killers; mental health, academic, and other experts who have studied serial killers and shared their expertise through education and publication; officers of the court, who have judged, prosecuted, and defended serial killers; and members of the media, who inform and educate the public when serial killers strike. The attendees also reflected the international nature of the serial murder problem, as there were attendees from ten different countries on five continents.

The agenda encompassed a variety of topics related to serial murder including common myths, definitions, typologies, pathology and causality, forensics, the role of the media, prosecution issues, investigative task force organization, and major case management issues. Each day included panel discussions, case presentations, and discussion groups addressing a range of topics related to serial murder.

This monograph is a culmination of the input and discussion of the attendees on the major issues related to serial murder. The contents are based upon the notes taken during the presentations, panel discussions, and break-out group sessions. The goal in publishing this monograph is to outline the consensus views from a variety of disciplines on the causality, motivations, and characteristics of serial murderers, which will enable the criminal justice community to generate a more effective response in the identification, investigation, and adjudication of these cases.

In: Serial Murderers
Editor: James T. Lawson, pp. 7-8
ISBN: 978-1-60692-204-0

NATIONAL CENTER FOR THE ANALYSIS OF VIOLENT CRIME

The National Center for the Analysis of Violent Crime (NCAVC) is a component of the FBI's Critical Incident Response Group (CIRG), located at the FBI Academy in Quantico, Virginia. The primary mission of the NCAVC is to provide behaviorally-based, operational support to federal, state, local, and international law enforcement agencies involved in the investigation of unusual or repetitive violent crimes, communicated threats, terrorism, and other matters of interest to law enforcement.

The NCAVC is comprised of four units: Behavioral Analysis Unit-1 (Counterterrorism/ Threat Assessment), Behavioral Analysis Unit-2 (Crimes Against Adults), Behavioral Analysis Unit-3 (Crimes Against Children), and the Violent Criminal Apprehension Program (ViCAP).

NCAVC staff members conduct detailed analyses of crimes from behavioral, forensic, and investigative perspectives. The goal of this analysis process is to provide law enforcement agencies with a better understanding of the motivations and behaviors of offenders. The analysis is a tool that provides investigators with descriptive and behavioral characteristics of the most probable offender and advice regarding investigative techniques to help identify the offender.

The NCAVC also conducts research into violent crime from a law enforcement perspective. NCAVC research is designed to gain insight into criminal thought processes, motivations, and behaviors. Research findings are refined into innovative, investigative techniques that improve law enforcement's effectiveness against violent criminals and are shared with law enforcement and other disciplines through publications, presentations, and training.

The Serial Murder Symposium was conceived, planned, and coordinated by the staff of the Behavioral Analysis Unit-2 (BAU-2). The resources of BAU-2 are focused on serial, mass, and other murders; sexual assaults; kidnappings; and other criminal acts targeting adult victims. BAU-2 staff members have developed significant expertise on the subject of serial murder and regularly provide operational assistance, conduct research, and provide training on issues related to serial murder.

In: Serial Murderers
Editor: James T. Lawson, pp. 9-14
ISBN: 978-1-60692-204-0

Chapter 1

INTRODUCTION

Serial murder is neither a new phenomenon, nor is it uniquely American. Dating back to ancient times, serial murderers have been chronicled around the world. In 19th century Europe, Dr. Richard von Krafft-Ebing conducted some of the first documented research on violent, sexual offenders and the crimes they committed. Best known for his 1886 textbook Psychopathia Sexualis, Dr. Kraft-Ebing described numerous case studies of sexual homicide, serial murder, and other areas of sexual proclivity.

Serial murder is a relatively rare event, estimated to comprise less than one percent of all murders committed in any given year. However, there is a macabre interest in the topic that far exceeds its scope and has generated countless articles, books, and movies. This broad-based public fascination began in the late 1880s, after a series of unsolved prostitute murders occurred in the Whitechapel area of London. These murders were committed by an unknown individual who named himself "Jack the Ripper" and sent letters to the police claiming to be the killer.

Dear Boss

I keep on hearing the police have caught me but they wont fix me just yet. I have laughed when they look so clever and talk about being on the right track. That joke about Leather Apron gave me real fits. I am down on whores and I shant quit ripping them till I do get buckled. Grand work the last job was. I gave the lady no time to squeal. How can they catch me now. I love my work and want to start again. You will soon hear of me with my funny little games. I saved some of the proper red stuff in a ginger beer bottle over the last job to write with but it went thick like glue and I cant use it. Red ink is fit enough I hope ha. ha. The next job I do I shall clip the ladys ears off and send to the police offi cers just for jolly wouldn't you. Keep this letter back till I do a bit more work, then give it out straight. My knife's so nice and sharp I want to get to work right away if I get a chance. Good luck. Yours truly Jack the Ripper

These murders and the nom de guerre "Jack the Ripper" have become synonymous with serial murder. This case spawned many legends concerning serial murder and the killers who commit it. In the 1970s and 1980s serial murder cases such as the Green River Killer, Ted Bundy, and BTK sparked a renewed public interest in serial murder, which blossomed in the 1990s after the release of films such as Silence of the Lambs.

Much of the general public's knowledge concerning serial murder is a product of Hollywood productions. Story lines are created to heighten the interest of audiences, rather than to accurately portray serial murder. By focusing on the atrocities inflicted on victims by "deranged" offenders, the public is captivated by the criminals and their crimes. This only lends more confusion to the true dynamics of serial murder.

Law enforcement professionals are subject to the same misinformation from a different source: the use of anecdotal information. Professionals involved in serial murder cases, such as investigators, prosecutors, and pathologists may have limited exposure to serial murder. Their experience may be based upon a single murder series, and the factors in that case are extrapolated to other serial murders. As a result, certain stereotypes and misconceptions take root regarding the nature of serial murder and the characteristics of serial killers.

A growing trend that compounds the fallacies surrounding serial murder is the talking heads phenomenon. Given creditability by the media, these self-proclaimed authorities profess to have an expertise in serial murder. They appear frequently on television and in the print media and speculate on the motive for the murders and the characteristics of the possible offender, without being privy to the facts of the investigation. Unfortunately, inappropriate comments may perpetuate misperceptions concerning serial murder and impair law enforcement's investigative efforts. It was decided by a majority of the attendees to issue a formal statement of position regarding the media's use of these types of individuals. (The position statement is included in Section X of this monograph.)

The relative rarity of serial murder combined with inaccurate, anecdotal information and fictional portrayals of serial killers has resulted in the following common myths and misconceptions regarding serial murder:

Myth: Serial killers are all dysfunctional loners

The majority of serial killers are not reclusive, social misfits who live alone. They are not monsters and may not appear strange. Many serial killers hide in plain sight within their communities. Serial murderers often have families and homes, are gainfully employed, and appear to be normal members of the community. Because many serial murderers can blend in so effortlessly, they are oftentimes overlooked by law enforcement and the public.

- Robert Yates killed seventeen prostitutes in the Spokane, Washington area, during the 1990s. He was married with five children, lived in a middle class neighborhood, and was a decorated U.S. Army National Guard helicopter pilot. During the time period of the murders, Yates routinely patronized prostitutes, and several of his victims knew each other. Yates buried one of his victims in his yard, beneath his bedroom window. Yates was eventually arrested and pled guilty to thirteen of the murders.
- The Green River Killer, Gary Ridgeway, confessed to killing 48 women over a twenty-year time period in the Seattle, Washington area. He had been married three times and was still married at the time of his arrest. He was employed as a truck painter for thirty-two years. He attended church regularly, read the Bible at home and at work, and talked about religion with co-workers. Ridgeway also frequently picked up prostitutes and had sex with them throughout the time period in which he was killing.
- The BTK killer, Dennis Rader, killed ten victims in and around Wichita, Kansas. He sent sixteen written communications to the news media over a thirty-year period, taunting the police and the public. He was married with two children, was a Boy Scout leader, served honorably in the U.S. Air Force, was employed as a local government official, and was president of his church.

Myth: Serial killers are all white males.

Contrary to popular belief, serial killers span all racial groups. There are white, African-American, Hispanic, and Asian serial killers. The racial diversification of serial killers generally mirrors that of the overall U.S. population.

- Charles Ng, a native of Hong Kong, China, killed numerous victims in Northern California, in concert with Robert Lake.
- Derrick Todd Lee, an African-American, killed at least six women in Baton Rouge, Louisiana.
- Coral Eugene Watts, an African-American, killed five victims in Michigan, fl ed the state to avoid detection, and murdered another 12 victims in Texas, before being apprehended.
- Rafael Resendez-Ramirez, a native of Mexico, murdered nine people in Kentucky, Texas, and Illinois, before turning himself in.
- Rory Conde, a Colombian native, was responsible for six prostitute homicides in the Miami, Florida area.

Myth: Serial killers are only motivated by sex.

All serial murders are not sexually-based. There are many other motivations for serial murders including anger, thrill, financial gain, and attention seeking.

- In the Washington, D.C. area serial sniper case, John Allen Muhammad, a former U.S. Army Staff Sergeant, and Lee Boyd Malvo killed primarily for anger and thrill motivations. They were able to terrorize the greater Washington, D.C. metro area for three weeks, shooting 13 victims, killing 10 of them. They communicated with the police by leaving notes, and they attempted to extort money to stop the shootings. They are suspected in a number of other shootings in seven other states.
- Dr. Michael Swango, a former U.S. Marine, ambulance worker, and physician, was a health care employee. He was convicted of only four murders in New York and Ohio, although he is suspected of having poisoned and killed 35 to 50 people throughout the United States and on the continent of Africa. Swango's motivation for the killings was intrinsic and never fully identified. Interestingly, Swango kept a scrap book fi lled with newspaper and magazine clippings about natural disasters, in which many people were killed.
- Paul Reid killed at least seven people during fast food restaurant robberies in Tennessee. After gaining control of the victims, he either stabbed or shot them. The motivation for the murders was primarily witness elimination. Reid's purpose in committing the robberies was financial gain, and some of the ill-gotten gains were used to purchase a car.

Myth: All serial murderers travel and operate interstate.

Most serial killers have very defined geographic areas of operation. They conduct their killings within comfort zones that are often defined by an anchor point (e.g. place of residence, employment, or residence of a relative). Serial murderers will, at times, spiral their activities outside of their comfort zone, when their confidence has grown through experience or to avoid detection. Very few serial murderers travel interstate to kill.

The few serial killers who do travel interstate to kill fall into a few categories:

- Itinerant individuals who move from place to place.
- Homeless individuals who are transients.
- Individuals whose employment lends itself to interstate or transnational travel, such as truck drivers or those in military service.

The difference between these types of offenders and other serial murderers is the nature of their traveling lifestyle, which provides them with many zones of comfort in which to operate.

Myth: Serial killers cannot stop killing.

It has been widely believed that once serial killers start killing, they cannot stop. There are, however, some serial killers who stop murdering altogether before being caught. In these instances, there are events or circumstances in offenders' lives that inhibit them from pursuing more victims. These can include increased participation in family activities, sexual substitution, and other diversions.

- BTK killer, Dennis Rader, murdered ten victims from 1974 to 1991. He did not kill any other victims prior to being captured in 2005. During interviews conducted by law enforcement, Rader admitted to engaging in auto-erotic activities as a substitute for his killings.
- Jeffrey Gorton killed his first victim in 1986 and his next victim in 1991. He did not kill another victim and was captured in 2002. Gorton engaged in cross-dressing and masturbatory activities, as well as consensual sex with his wife in the interim.

Myth: All Serial killers are insane or are evil geniuses.

Another myth that exists is that serial killers have either a debilitating mental condition, or they are extremely clever and intelligent.

As a group, serial killers suffer from a variety of personality disorders, including psychopathy, anti-social personality, and others. Most, however, are not adjudicated as insane under the law.

The media has created a number of fictional serial killer “geniuses”, who outsmart law enforcement at every turn. Like other populations, however, serial killers range in intelligence from borderline to above average levels.

Myth: Serial killers want to get caught.

Offenders committing a crime for the first time are inexperienced. They gain experience and confidence with each new offense, eventually succeeding with few mistakes or problems.

While most serial killers plan their offenses more thoroughly than other criminals, the learning curve is still very steep. They must select, target, approach, control, and dispose of their victims. The logistics involved in committing a murder and disposing of the body can become very complex, especially when there are multiple sites involved.

As serial killers continue to offend without being captured, they can become empowered, feeling they will never be identified. As the series continues, the killers may begin to take shortcuts when committing their crimes. This often causes the killers to take more chances, leading to identification by law enforcement. It is not that serial killers want to get caught; they feel that they can’t get caught.

In: Serial Murderers
Editor: James T. Lawson, pp. 15-17
ISBN: 978-1-60692-204-0

Chapter 2

DEFINITION OF SERIAL MURDER

In the past thirty years, multiple definitions of serial murder have been used by law enforcement, clinicians, academia, and researchers. While these definitions do share several common themes, they differ on specific requirements, such as the number of murders involved, the types of motivation, and the temporal aspects of the murders. To address these discrepancies, attendees at the Serial Murder Symposium examined the variations in order to develop a single definition for serial murder.

Previous definitions of serial murder specified a certain number of murders, varying from two to ten victims. This quantitative requirement distinguished a serial murder from other categories of murder (i.e. single, double, or triple murder).

Most of the definitions also required a period of time between the murders. This break-in-time was necessary to distinguish between a mass murder and a serial murder. Serial murder required a temporal separation between the different murders, which was described as: separate occasions, cooling-off period, and emotional cooling-off period.

Generally, mass murder was described as a number of murders (four or more) occurring during the same incident, with no distinctive time period between the murders. These events typically involved a single location, where the killer murdered a number of victims in an ongoing incident (e.g. the 1984 San Ysidro McDonalds incident in San Diego, California; the 1991 Luby's Restaurant massacre in Killeen, Texas; and the 2007 Virginia Tech murders in Blacksburg, Virginia).

There has been at least one attempt to formalize a definition of serial murder through legislation. In 1998, a federal law was passed by the United States

Congress, titled: Protection of Children from Sexual Predator Act of 1998 (Title 18, United States Code, Chapter 51, and Section 1111). This law includes a definition of serial killings:

The term 'serial killings' means a series of three or more killings, not less than one of which was committed within the United States, having common characteristics such as to suggest the reasonable possibility that the crimes were committed by the same actor or actors.

Although the federal law provides a definition of serial murder, it is limited in its application. The purpose of this definition was to set forth criteria establishing when the FBI could assist local law enforcement agencies with their investigation of serial murder cases. It was not intended to be a generic definition for serial murder.

The Symposium attendees reviewed the previous definitions and extensively discussed the pros and cons of the numerous variations. The consensus of the Symposium attendees was to create a simple but broad definition, designed for use primarily by law enforcement.

One discussion topic focused on the determination of the number of murders that constituted a serial murder. Academicians and researchers were interested in establishing a specific number of murders, to allow clear inclusion criteria for their research on serial killers. However, since the definition was to be utilized by law enforcement, a lower number of victims would allow law enforcement more flexibility in committing resources to a potential serial murder investigation.

Motivation was another central element discussed in various definitions; however, attendees felt motivation did not belong in a general definition, as it would make the defi nition overly complex.

The validity of spree murder as a separate category was discussed at great length. The general definition of spree murder is two or more murders committed by an offender or offenders, without a cooling-off period. According to the definition, the lack of a cooling-off period marks the difference between a spree murder and a serial murder. Central to the discussion was the definitional problems relating to the concept of a cooling-off period. Because it creates arbitrary guidelines, the confusion surrounding this concept led the majority of attendees to advocate disregarding the use of spree murder as a separate category. The designation does not provide any real benefit for use by law enforcement.

The different discussion groups at the Symposium agreed on a number of similar factors to be included in a definition. These included:

- one or more offenders
- two or more murdered victims

- incidents should be occurring in separate events, at different times
- the time period between murders separates serial murder from mass murder

In combining the various ideas put forth at the Symposium, the following definition was crafted:

Serial Murder: The unlawful killing of two or more victims by the same offender(s), in separate events.

In: Serial Murderers
Editor: James T. Lawson, pp. 19-20
ISBN: 978-1-60692-204-0

Chapter 3

CAUSALITY AND THE SERIAL MURDERER

Following the arrest of a serial killer, the question is always asked: How did this person become a serial murderer? The answer lies in the development of the individual from birth to adulthood. Specifically, the behavior a person displays is influenced by life experiences, as well as certain biological factors. Serial murderers, like all human beings, are the product of their heredity, their upbringing, and the choices they make throughout development. Causality, as it relates to the development of serial murderers, was discussed at length by the Symposium attendees.

Causality can be defined as a complex process based on biological, social, and environmental factors. In addition to these factors, individuals have the ability to choose to engage in certain behaviors. The collective outcome of all of these infl uences separates individual behavior from generic human behavior. Since it is not possible to identify all of the factors that influence normal human behavior, it similarly is not possible to identify all of the factors that influence an individual to become a serial murderer.

Human beings are in a constant state of development from the moment of conception until death. Behavior is affected by stimulation received and processed by the central nervous system. Neurobiologists believe that our nervous systems are environmentally sensitive, thereby allowing individual nervous systems to be shaped throughout a lifetime.

The development of social coping mechanisms begins early in life and continues to progress as children learn to interact, negotiate, and compromise with their peers. In some individuals the failure to develop adequate coping mechanisms results in violent behavior.

Neglect and abuse in childhood have been shown to contribute to an increased risk of future violence. Substance abuse can and does lead to increased aggression and violence. There are documented cases of people who suffered severe head injuries and ultimately become violent, even when there was no prior history of violence.

Symposium attendees agreed that there is no single identifiable cause or factor that leads to the development of a serial killer. Rather, there are a multitude of factors that contribute to their development. The most signifi cant factor is the serial killer's personal decision in choosing to pursue their crimes.

There were several additional observations made by the attendees regarding causality:

- Predisposition to serial killing, much like other violent offenses, is biological, social, and psychological in nature, and it is not limited to any specific characteristic or trait.
- The development of a serial killer involves a combination of these factors, which exist together in a rare confluence in certain individuals. They have the appropriate biological predisposition, molded by their psychological makeup, which is present at a critical time in their social development.
- There are no specific combinations of traits or characteristics shown to differentiate serial killers from other violent offenders.
- There is no generic template for a serial killer.
- Serial killers are driven by their own unique motives or reasons.
- Serial killers are not limited to any specific demographic group, such as their sex, age, race, or religion.
- The majority of serial killers who are sexually motivated erotized violence during development. For them, violence and sexual gratification are inexplicably intertwined in their psyche.
- More research is needed to identify specific pathways of development that produce serial killers.

In: Serial Murderers
Editor: James T. Lawson, pp. 21-22
ISBN: 978-1-60692-204-0

Chapter 4

PSYCHOPATHY AND SERIAL MURDER

Attendees at the Serial Murder Symposium agreed that there is no generic profile of a serial murderer. Serial killers differ in many ways, including their motivations for killing and their behavior at the crime scene. However, attendees did identify certain traits common to some serial murderers, including sensation seeking, a lack of remorse or guilt, impulsivity, the need for control, and predatory behavior. These traits and behaviors are consistent with the psychopathic personality disorder. Attendees felt it was very important for law enforcement and other professionals in the criminal justice system to understand psychopathy and its relationship to serial murder.

Psychopathy is a personality disorder manifested in people who use a mixture of charm, manipulation, intimidation, and occasionally violence to control others, in order to satisfy their own selfish needs. Although the concept of psychopathy has been known for centuries, Dr. Robert Hare led the modern research effort to develop a series of assessment tools, to evaluate the personality traits and behaviors attributable to psychopaths.

Dr. Hare and his associates developed the Psychopathy Check List Revised (PCL-R) and its derivatives, which provide a clinical assessment of the degree of psychopathy an individual possesses. These instruments measure the distinct cluster of personality traits and socially-deviant behaviors of an individual, which fall into four factors: interpersonal, affective, lifestyle, and anti-social.

The interpersonal traits include glibness, superficial charm, a grandiose sense of self-worth, pathological lying, and the manipulation of others. The affective traits include a lack of remorse and/or guilt, shallow affect, a lack of empathy, and failure to accept responsibility. The lifestyle behaviors include stimulation-seeking behavior, impulsivity, irresponsibility, parasitic orientation, and a lack of realistic life goals. The anti-social behaviors include poor behavioral controls, early childhood behavior problems, juvenile delinquency, revocation of conditional release, and criminal versatility. The combination of these individual personality traits, interpersonal styles, and socially deviant lifestyles are the framework of psychopathy and can manifest themselves differently in individual psychopaths.

Research has demonstrated that in those offenders who are psychopathic, scores vary, ranging from a high degree of psychopathy to some measure of psychopathy. However, not all violent offenders are psychopaths and not all psychopaths are violent offenders. If violent offenders are psychopathic, they are able to assault, rape, and murder without concern for legal, moral, or social consequences. This allows them to do what they want, whenever they want.

The relationship between psychopathy and serial killers is particularly interesting. All psychopaths do not become serial murderers. Rather, serial murderers may possess some or many of the traits consistent with psychopathy. Psychopaths who commit serial murder do not value human life and are extremely callous in their interactions with their victims. This is particularly evident in sexually motivated serial killers who repeatedly target, stalk, assault, and kill without a sense of remorse. However, psychopathy alone does not explain the motivations of a serial killer.

Understanding psychopathy becomes particularly critical to law enforcement during a serial murder investigation and upon the arrest of a psychopathic serial killer. The crime scene behavior of psychopaths is likely to be distinct from other offenders. This distinct behavior can assist law enforcement in linking serial cases.

Psychopaths are not sensitive to altruistic interview themes, such as sympathy for their victims or remorse/guilt over their crimes. They do possess certain personality traits that can be exploited, particularly their inherent narcissism, selfishness, and vanity. Specific themes in past successful interviews of psychopathic serial killers focused on praising their intelligence, cleverness, and skill in evading capture.

Attendees recognized that more research is needed concerning the links between serial murder and psychopathy, in order to understand the frequency and degree of psychopathy among serial murderers. This may assist law enforcement in understanding and identifying serial murderers.

In: Serial Murderers
Editor: James T. Lawson, pp. 23-25
ISBN: 978-1-60692-204-0

Chapter 5

MOTIVATIONS AND TYPES OF SERIAL MURDER: THE SYMPOSIUM MODEL

Over the past twenty years, law enforcement and experts from a number of varying disciplines have attempted to identify specific motivations for serial murderers and to apply those motivations to different typologies developed for classifying serial murderers. These range from simple, definitive models to complex, multiple-category typologies that are laden with inclusion requirements. Most typologies are too cumbersome to be utilized by law enforcement during an active serial murder investigation, and they may not be helpful in identifying an offender.

The attendees at the Symposium discussed the issues surrounding motivation and the use of typologies to categorize varying types of serial murder. Identifying motivations in the investigation of a crime is a standard procedure for law enforcement. Typically, motivation provides police with the means to narrow the potential suspect pool.

The same logical steps are taken when investigating homicide cases. As most homicides are committed by someone known to the victim, police focus on the relationships closest to the victim. This is a successful strategy for most murder investigations. The majority of serial murderers, however, are not acquainted with or involved in a consensual relationship with their victims.

For the most part, serial murder involves strangers with no visible relationship between the offender and the victim. This distinguishes a serial murder investigation as a more nebulous undertaking than that of other crimes. Since the investigations generally lack an obvious connection between the offender and the victim, investigators instead attempt to discern the motivations behind the murders, as a way to narrow their investigative focus.

Serial murder crime scenes can have bizarre features that may cloud the identifi cation of a motive. The behavior of a serial murderer at crime scenes may evolve throughout the series of crimes and manifest different interactions between an offender and a victim. It is also extremely difficult to identify a single motivation when there is more than one offender involved in the series.

The attendees at the Symposium made the following observations:

- Motive generally may be difficult to determine in a serial murder investigation.
- A serial murderer may have multiple motives for committing his crimes.
- A serial murderer's motives may evolve both within a single murder as well throughout the murder series.
- The classification of motivations should be limited to observable behavior at the crime scene.
- Even if a motive can be Identified, it may not be helpful in identifying a serial murderer.
- Utilizing investigative resources to discern the motive instead of identifying the offender may derail the investigation.
- Investigators should not necessarily equate a serial murderer's motivation with the level of injury.
- Regardless of the motive, serial murderers commit their crimes because they want to. The exception to this would be those few killers suffering from a severe mental illness.

To assist law enforcement in narrowing the pool of suspects, attendees at the Symposium suggested that broad, non-inclusive categories of motivations be utilized as guidelines for investigation. The following categories listed below represent general categories and are not intended to be a complete measure of serial offenders or their motivation:

- *Anger* is a motivation in which an offender displays rage or hostility towards a certain subgroup of the population or with society as a whole.
- *Criminal Enterprise* is a motivation in which the offender benefits in status or monetary compensation by committing murder that is drug, gang, or organized crime related.
- *Financial gain* is a motivation in which the offender benefits monetarily from killing. Examples of these types of crimes are "black widow" killings, robbery homicides, or multiple killings involving insurance or welfare fraud.

- *Ideology* is a motivation to commit murders in order to further the goals and ideas of a specific individual or group. Examples of these include terrorist groups or an individual(s) who attacks a specific racial, gender, or ethnic group.
- *Power/thrill* is a motivation in which the offender feels empowered and/or excited when he kills his victims.
- *Psychosis* is a situation in which the offender is suffering from a severe mental illness and is killing because of that illness. This may include auditory and/or visual hallucinations and paranoid, grandiose, or bizarre delusions.
- *Sexually-based* is a motivation driven by the sexual needs/desires of the offender. There may or may not be overt sexual contact reflected in the crime scene.

An offender selects a victim, regardless of the category, based upon availability, vulnerability, and desirability. Availability is explained as the lifestyle of the victim or circumstances in which the victim is involved, that allow the offender access to the victim. Vulnerability is defined as the degree to which the victim is susceptible to attack by the offender. Desirability is described as the appeal of the victim to the offender. Desirability involves numerous factors based upon the motivation of the offender and may include factors dealing with the race, gender, ethnic background, age of the victim, or other specific preferences the offender determines.

In: Serial Murderers
Editor: James T. Lawson, pp. 27-37
ISBN: 978-1-60692-204-0

Chapter 6

INVESTIGATIVE ISSUES AND BEST PRACTICES

Attendees at the Symposium identified successful investigative practices for solving serial murder cases. These factors were central to the discussions:

- Identification of a Serial Murder Series
- Leadership
- Task Force Organization
- Resource Augmentation
- Communication
- Data Management
- Analytical Tools
- Medical Examiners/Coroners
- Administrative Issues
- Training
- Offi cer Assistance Programs

IDENTIFICATION

Symposium participants listed the initial identification of a homicide series as the primary investigative challenge. Historically, the first indication that a serial murderer was at work was when two or more cases were linked by forensic or behavioral evidence.

Identifying a homicide series is easier in rapidly-developing, high profile cases involving low risk victims. These cases are reported to law enforcement upon discovery of the crimes and draw immediate media attention.

In contrast, identifying a series involving high risk victims in multiple jurisdictions is much more difficult. This is primarily due to the high risk lifestyle and transitory nature of the victims. Additionally, the lack of communication between law enforcement agencies and differing records management systems impede the linkage of cases to a common offender.

Attendees stressed the importance of law enforcement networking with other investigative agencies and cited the National Law Enforcement Teletype System (NLETS) messages, ViCAP Alerts, and the Law Enforcement Online (LEO) website as alternative mechanisms for sharing information to help determine other linked cases. The use of the FBI's NCAVC, both the Behavioral Analysis Units and the Violent Criminal Apprehension Program, in linking potential cases was also encouraged.

LEADERSHIP

High profile investigations present a multitude of leadership challenges for law enforcement, from investigators to police executives. Law enforcement personnel may face external pressures from political entities, victims' families, and the media. Collectively, strong management throughout the chain of command must continually reinforce the supreme goal of the investigation: To arrest and prosecute the offender.

Attendees at the Symposium agreed that in successful serial murder investigations, the roles of both investigators and supervisors were clearly delineated. The investigative function is the primary mission, and all other activities are in support of that mission.

In serial murder cases, the actual investigation should be directed by competent, homicide investigators, who have the experience to direct and focus the investigative process. Law enforcement administrators should not run the investigation but rather ensure that the investigators have the resources to do their job. Supervisors should also act as buffers between investigators and the other levels of command.

There are several other strategies law enforcement executives may consider while preparing for these intense investigations:

- Completing Memorandums of Understanding (MOUs) between different law enforcement agencies, in order to obtain mutual support agreements and commitment of manpower, resources, and overtime.
- Identifying all resources that may be needed during the investigation and maintaining detailed lists of available resources.
- Establishing good working relationships with other departments prior to the crisis, through networking, scheduled meetings, and joint training.
- Providing training opportunities in the latest techniques and methods of homicide investigation.

Additional observations regarding leadership in task force operations include:

- Communication on administrative issues should be restricted to management personnel of the various agencies, so as not to distract investigators.
- The intense pressure in high profile investigations may at times decrease logical decision making. Tunnel vision and impulsivity should be avoided.
- Law enforcement administration in each of the participating law enforcement agencies should present a unified front by agreeing to a written investigative strategy that outlines the investigative goals, the roles of the agencies, and establishes a clear and concise chain of command.
- Command staff should focus on providing and managing the resources investigators need to solve the case, rather than directing the investigation. A major problem identified by attendees at the Symposium was the issue of micro-management. When a supervisor attempts to personally direct every action in an investigation, rather than allowing investigators to perform their jobs independently, they exacerbate problems in these high profile investigations.
- While law enforcement attracts positive individuals with strong personalities, management should encourage all involved personnel to leave their "egos" at the door. This ensures that personality differences among investigators do not become a distraction to the investigation. Investigators who lack the ability to collaborate with colleagues can hinder the investigation and should not be assigned to investigative teams.

Task Force Organization

Once a serial murder series has been identified, it is important for the involved law enforcement agencies to work together. There are a number of operational and investigative issues critical to the successful establishment of an investigative task force.

Initially, a lead agency for the task force should be designated and will assume the primary investigative role. The choice of a lead agency is based upon a number of factors including the number and viability of the cases, available resources, and investigative experience. Once established, all law enforcement agencies involved in the investigation should have representation in the task force. Any outlying agencies should also be included, even if they do not have an identified case in the investigation.

An effective and reliable investigative model identifies a lead investigator and coinvestigator, who, regardless of rank, are given complete control of the investigation. These investigators review all incoming information, collate the information, and assign leads. If the flow of incoming information becomes unmanageable due to an excessive influx of investigative tips, the lead investigators can delegate this responsibility to an experienced investigator, who will act as a lead control offi cer. Administrators must look beyond the traditional method of assigning the next available investigators regardless of skill or assigning investigators who have no desire to be involved in a major case. Consequently, law enforcement administrators must assign the most qualified investigator(s) to lead the current case.

The lead investigator(s) must have the experience, dedication, and tenacity to direct all aspects of the investigation. They should also, with management's support, have the ability to select a cadre of investigators and support personnel and assign such personnel as the investigation dictates. In serial murder investigations, the lead investigators must handle all crime scene activities and related leads, as each incident may be interwoven. It is the responsibility of the lead investigators or the lead control investigator to ensure relevant information is distributed to the entire task force.

At the onset of the task force, the lead investigators should immediately implement a preplanned task force model. Common to most models is the need to establish an information management system to track tips and leads in the case. This computer system should account for the idiosyncrasies of the investigation while being flexible enough to handle any contingency. All personnel should be familiar with its operation, and it should be pre-tested to insure viability in investigative conditions.

Primary to the investigation is sufficient manpower to successfully investigate and prosecute the case. The overwhelming consensus from the attendees is that the assignment of excessive numbers of personnel to the investigation may be counterproductive. A small group of experienced homicide investigators, under the direction of the lead investigator(s), is far more effective than a large number of less experienced investigators or investigators who are experienced in different areas of criminal activity. Additional personnel may be brought in for specific tasks as necessary.

There should be a bifurcation of responsibility between the administration of the case and the investigation of the case. The task of running the investigation is the responsibility of the lead investigator. The administration provides all of the necessary support, including procurement of equipment, funding, and manpower. As an example, task force administrators must obtain authority for priority requests for services, from the forensic laboratory and other service providers. The lead investigator(s) and the administrators of the task force must have a close, cooperative working relationship, while maintaining their own areas of responsibility.

Assignment of liaison personnel in serial homicide cases is highly recommended. The highest priority is the families of the victims, who will be supportive of the investigative efforts, when they believe the investigators are competent and all available resources are being used to identify and arrest the offender. An investigator with exceptional interpersonal and communication skills should be assigned to maintain constant contact with the families, keeping them apprised of the progress of the investigation and any pending press releases.

Liaison must also be maintained with the numerous support entities both inside and outside the task force including the prosecutor's office, the forensic laboratory, the medical examiner's office, and surrounding law enforcement agencies. Additionally, a list of available experts in specific forensic and related fields should be compiled and liaison established for use in the investigation. As long as the flow of information is manageable, one individual can be assigned to multiple liaison duties.

Resource Augmentation

As the investigation continues, the manpower requirements of the task force will increase for various reasons, including increasing the number of investigators and support staff. Restraint must be practiced by task force administrators to avoid the use of excess personnel. As previously discussed, the use of fewer personnel may be more effective. The lead investigator is in the best position to recognize when additional personnel are needed. The administrator's responsibility is to provide the authority for the permanent or temporary reassignment of the requested number of personnel to the task force.

If additional personnel are needed to expand the task force, the reassignment should be for the duration of the task force, to insure continuity of investigative information. However, for short term needs such as a specific neighborhood canvass or road block canvass, personnel can be reassigned temporarily to complete the specific task and then be returned to their normal duties.

In either event, the arrival of new personnel should be preplanned and a detailed case briefing provided. This briefing should include an explanation of their specific assignment, their work hours, details of the investigation as it applies to their assignment, expected standards for report completion, and a complete list of contact numbers. Additionally, personnel should be cautioned about discussing case sensitive information with anyone outside of authorized law enforcement personnel.

Arbitrary rotation of personnel should be avoided, as it negatively affects the continuity of the investigation. Rotation of personnel should only occur if requested by the investigator, or there are officer assistance issues. If the task force is disbanded and later reinstated, the original investigators should be utilized.

COMMUNICATIONS

Attendees stressed the importance of disseminating information to the investigators engaged in a serial murder investigation through the following:

- Daily briefings are essential for investigators, especially when there are different work shifts. Periodic summary briefings are also necessary for managers and patrol officers. These can be accomplished via e-mails or at roll call and should be conducted by investigative personnel.
- Communication on the operational level is paramount, especially in task force investigations and when serial murder cases involve multiple states. As all information must be shared seamlessly, teleconferences may not sufficiently allow for the flow of information. Face-to-face case briefings are suggested.
- Submitting ViCAP reports on solved and unsolved murders, attempted murders, and sexual assaults for inclusion in the ViCAP database is

strongly recommended and may facilitate the linkage of unknown related cases for law enforcement agencies.

Data Management

A common problem in serial investigations occurs when data is not entered into the electronic database in a timely manner. Useful leads are lost when investigators are overloaded with information. The following suggestions were provided regarding data management issues:

- In order to avoid time lags, reports should be written as soon as the investigative lead is completed. If reports are not finished before the end of the investigator's shift, the lead investigator(s) may not have time to review those reports. This will lead to a back-log of reports, containing pertinent and timely investigative information.
- Sufficient time should be allocated during work shifts to complete reports.
- Information should be obtained, documented, and distributed in a standardized manner, to maintain consistency among different agencies. Ideally, reports should be computer generated to ease the communication issues.
- Systems similar to the FBI's Rapid Start computerized case management system should be utilized, to effectively organize and collate lead information. Computerized systems promote the analysis of a tremendous amount of data. There should be sufficient personnel committed to ensure that data is recorded into the system, in a timely manner.
- A murder book or series of murder books should be created and maintained. Murder books contain all of the pertinent investigative information and are traditionally in paper format but can also be developed electronically.
- All rough notes should be maintained and entered into evidence.
- Reports should be distributed to all participating law enforcement agencies and the prosecutor's office.

Analytical Tools

The wide range of analytical resources available to law enforcement agencies is typically under-utilized at the onset of a serial murder investigation. Due to the voluminous amount of information characteristic of high profile investigations, critical lead information may be lost. The implementation of a tested and reliable case management system, as previously discussed, coupled with competent analytical staff, is imperative in serial murder investigations.

Crime analysts offer critical support to the investigation by developing timelines on victims and suspects, compiling matrices to highlight similar case elements, and providing general analytical support. Analysts should be assigned to the initial investigation group, so information can be sorted, compared, and charted to provide timely lead information.

It is recommended that a review team of experienced investigators be formed to assist the lead investigator(s) in filtering through the information gathered by analysts. The team should consist of two to four investigators from within the involved agencies, as well as the crime analysts. The team must remain intact throughout the investigation, to maintain the case integrity.

Many agencies are not supported by an actual crime analysis unit or do not employ experienced analysts. In such cases, the agency should contact their neighboring jurisdictions or the FBI's National Center for the Analysis of Violent Crime for assistance.

Symposium attendees also discussed the importance of the behavioral aspects of the investigation and recommended the FBI's Behavioral Analysis Unit be utilized for the multitude of services it provides to include crime scene analysis, offender profi les, case linkage analysis, interview strategies, and prosecution strategy. The case consultations can be conducted at the BAU office in Quantico, Virginia, or a team of BAU staff members can respond to the respective agency, to personally view the crime scenes and discuss the behavioral issues with the pertinent task force members.

Medical Examiners/Coroners

A thorough autopsy and the subsequent collection of evidence are critical in serial murder investigations. Medical examiners and coroners operate according to their different state mandates and vary as to the thoroughness of their investigations. Consistent procedures to collect, record, and retrieve case information are important in linking cases in other jurisdictions.

The following recommendations were made concerning medical examiners in serial murder investigations:

- Medical examiners should share information on autopsies in potentially related cases. Joint meetings with investigators can provide additional background information on these cases.
- A single medical examiner should be utilized in serial cases occurring within the same jurisdiction.
- Once a series has been identified that involves several jurisdictions, the various medical examiner offices may consider performing joint autopsy procedures to ensure continuity in evidence collection.
- Investigators should also ensure submissions of all unidentified victims to the FBI Laboratory's National Missing Persons DNA database.
- Investigators should also ensure the entry of unidentified remains recovered into the National Crime Information Center (NCIC) and ViCAP.

Administrative Issues

Law enforcement agencies should review their current administrative policies relating to maintenance and storage of unsolved homicide case materials. Top priority should be given to these cases by extending the storage time limit and may include the following:

- Mirror the FBI's NCAVC 50-year minimum mandate to keep copies of all unsolved cases.
- Retain records of unsolved homicide cases and the accompanying evidence until the case is closed.
- Records should be electronically converted.
- Evidence storage should be available for long term storage of forensic evidence in murder cases.
- Submit cases to the FBI's ViCAP database, which maintains case information indefi nitely.

Resources and Finances

It is essential that an investigative agency have the resources available in order to establish the initial setup for a task force, both from financial and logistic perspectives.

There should be a contingency plan in place to handle the resource issues in a major investigation. Buildings, office space, computers, phones, vehicles, food, and other necessities should be considered in the plan.

Utilizing non-law enforcement agencies, such as the fire department for use of their high-tech equipment, may also be included in the plan. It was recommended that agencies develop emergency response plans and establish MOU's at the local, state, and national level.

Training

Training continues to be an issue for all law enforcement departments. Complex homicide investigations, especially those involving serial murder cases, depend upon the experience and abilities of investigators to effectively conduct the investigation. With the retirement of many experienced homicide investigators, newer investigators need training and exposure to a wide range of investigative techniques. Attendees also suggested the utilization of standardized training for homicide investigators, crime analysts, and medical examiners.

Officer Assistance Programs

The brutality of the crime scenes; the senseless, repetitive acts inflicted on the victims; and a sense of helplessness in failing to catch the offender are all factors that may impact the emotional well-being of investigators involved in a serial murder case. Burnout, stress, and hopelessness are just some of the feelings that may affect members of the investigative team.

To combat these issues, attendees suggested the following:

- Regular debriefings.
- Access to critical incident counselors.
- Mental health evaluations upon request.
- Adequate time off for investigators.

NOTE: The majority of attendees agreed there should be a published, general guide to serial murder investigations, building upon the Multi-Agency Investigative Team Manual (MAIT) and addressing specific issues such as cooperative investigative models; investigative methods; case linkage; crime scene techniques; MOUs; training for police, medical examiners, and crime analysts; the role of regional intelligence centers; the integration of BAU and ViCAP; and the role of federal law enforcement.

In: Serial Murderers
Editor: James T. Lawson, pp. 39-44
ISBN: 978-1-60692-204-0

Chapter 7

FORENSIC ISSUES IN SERIAL MURDER CASES

The forensic sciences have played a key role in criminal investigations for many years. Recently, there has been increased attention on the forensic sciences by law enforcement, prosecutors, and the general public. Particularly in high profile cases, intense media coverage concerning evidence issues and the work of crime laboratories has served to heighten this interest.

In the past two decades, there have been tremendous technological advances in the laboratory testing of forensic samples. There have also been a number of improvements in the identification and collection of evidence at the crime scene, through innovative processing and evidence collection methods. Together, these advances allow for a greater probability of successful recovery and analysis of evidence than was previously possible. There is also growing recognition by criminal justice professionals of the wider scope of forensic techniques and available tests.

The field of forensic deoxyribonucleic acid (DNA) analysis and the legislation that allows DNA testing on a broader number of offenders has made some of the more remarkable advances. DNA testing now allows much smaller samples of biological material to be analyzed and the results to be more discriminating. DNA testing of forensic crime scene samples can now be compared against a database of known offenders and other unsolved crimes.

Forensic laboratories have developed advanced analytical techniques through the use of computer technology. Systems such as the Combined DNA Index System (CODIS), various Automated Fingerprint Identification Systems (AFIS), and the National Integrated Ballistics Identification Network (NIBIN), were identified by the symposium as beneficial to serial murder investigations, by providing links between previously unrelated cases.

CODIS is a national automated DNA information processing and telecommunications system that was developed to link biological evidence (DNA) in criminal cases, between various jurisdictions around the United States. Samples in CODIS include DNA profiles obtained from persons convicted of designated crimes, DNA profiles obtained from crime scenes, DNA profiles from unidentified human remains, and DNA from voluntary samples taken from families of missing persons.

30The CODIS data bank of these samples is comprised of three different indices or levels: the National DNA Index System (NDIS), the State DNA Index System (SDIS), and the Local DNA Index System (LDIS).

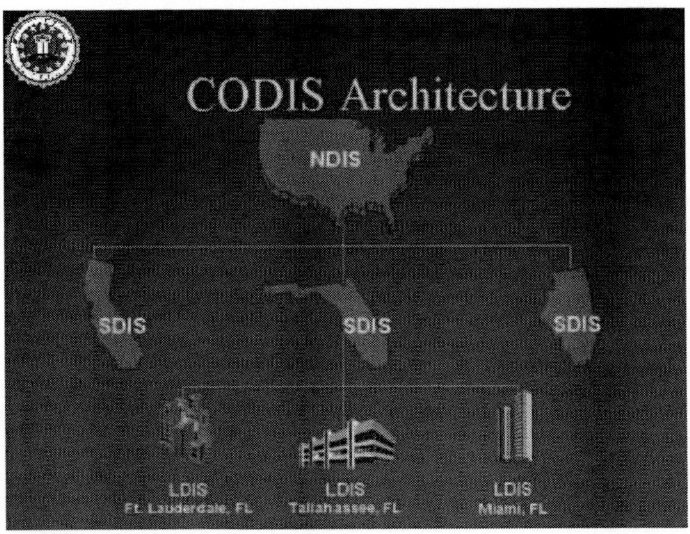

What is important for law enforcement to understand is that the information contained at the LDIS and SDIS levels may not automatically be sent to, or searched against, the NDIS level. There are different legislation requirements for inclusion into NDIS, than to LDIS or SDIS, and not all LDIS and SDIS profi les are sent to NDIS. Even when NDIS is queried, individual SDIS data banks may not be queried. Therefore, when dealing with a serial murder case, investigators need to contact their LDIS or SDIS level representatives to ensure that in addition to the NDIS databank, samples are compared in the individual SDIS data banks of each state that is of investigative interest. In cases where there is only a partial DNA profi le, a national "keyboard" search can be requested through the NDIS custodian, CODIS Unit, FBI Laboratory. AFIS is an electronic databank that compares unidentifi ed latent and patent fi ngerprints to the known fi ngerprint fi le. There have been a variety of local AFIS systems in use since the 1980s. In 1999, the FBI's Integrated Automated Fingerprint Identifi cation System, or IAFIS, became operational. IAFIS is designated as the national repository of criminal histories, fi ngerprints, and photographs of criminal subjects in the United States. It also contains fi ngerprints and information on military and civilian federal employees. IAFIS provides positive identification through comparisons of individuals based on the submission of fingerprint data, through both ten-print fingerprint cards and latent fingerprints.

Some of the earlier AFIS systems were not compatible with the IAFIS system, and as a result, those earlier latent fingerprints may not be included in IAFIS. This becomes an issue in serial murder cases, when the offender committed offenses prior to the inception of IAFIS, as latent fingerprints from those earlier crimes will not be searchable. If there is a possibility the offender committed early crimes, the early AFIS systems need to be queried independently. Consultation with laboratory fingerprint experts may be necessary in order to establish what AFIS systems exist, which are interoperable, and the protocols required to query each system.

NIBIN is a national databank of both projectile and cartridge information. NIBIN is the integration of two previous systems: the FBI's Drugfire cartridge case imaging system and the Bureau of Alcohol, Tobacco, Firearms and Explosives' (ATF) Integrated Ballistic Identification System (IBIS). NIBIN is an imaging system that allows both bullets and cartridges recovered from a crime scene to be compared electronically against other bullets and cartridges recovered from previous crime scenes, in an effort to link previously unrelated cases. The system can search by geographic area or nationwide, depending upon the course of the investigation. ATF is maintaining the new system in over 75 locations, across the United States.

When conducting serial murder investigations, it is important for investigators to promptly seek guidance from appropriate forensic database experts. Such experts can provide information regarding what limitations exist and what additional queries can be made of the systems, to obtain additional investigative information.

Another area in which forensic science can play an important role is in the recovery and examination of trace evidence. Trace evidence is described as small, often microscopic material. It commonly includes hair and fiber evidence but may encompass almost any substance or material. Trace evidence may provide important lead information pertaining to offender characteristics, vehicle and tire descriptors, and environmental clues that relate to killing scenes and modes of transportation used to move bodies.

A skilled trace evidence examiner can compare the trace evidence from all of the victims in a serial murder case, in an effort to identify evidence common to all of the victims. This trace evidence will reflect a "common environment" with which all of the victims were in contact. This common environment will repeat in objects in the serial offender's world, such as his vehicles and/or residence. This can demonstrate that all of the victims had contact with the offender at the same location(s).

Attendees at the Serial Murder Symposium universally acknowledged that serial murder cases present unique circumstances and concerns, particularly when multiple investigative jurisdictions are involved. In serial murder cases, crime scenes may occur in different law enforcement jurisdictions, each of whom may possess varying resources and abilities to process crime scenes. In some cases, agencies submit evidence to different laboratories, even though those agencies are located adjacent to one another. These issues degrade the ability of law enforcement to consistently collect evidence from a murder series. This may prevent identifying a serial killer or forensically linking previously unrelated cases to a common offender.

Attendees identified a number of forensic issues facing the law enforcement community in serial murder investigations and made the following suggestions:

- Once a series is identified, the same crime scene personnel should be utilized at related scenes to promote consistency in evidence identification and collection. Search personnel should follow established sterilization procedures to ensure there is no cross-contamination between the various crime scenes.
- Cross-contamination should be proactively prevented by using different personnel to process crime scenes than those used to collect known sample evidence from potential suspects.
- Documentation among the law enforcement agencies should be standardized to ensure continuity between separate cases.
- Aerial photographs of every murder crime scene, as well as the accompanying ancillary scenes, should be taken. Aerial photographs clearly depict the geography of the area and demonstrate the physical relationships and the distances between the crime scenes. They also identify potential routes of ingress and egress to the area.
- The number of laboratories and experts involved in serial murder investigations should be limited to properly certified facilities and

personnel. expert per discipline. If this is not possible, establish lines of communication between laboratories to ensure the sharing of pertinent information related to the investigation.

- Priority status for laboratory examinations should be obtained to ensure a quick turn around on test results.
- When consulting with forensic scientists, investigators should prioritize forensic examinations based upon their potential investigative value. In addition, forensic scientists should be consulted frequently to identify alternative sampling and/or testing that may lead to successful case resolution.
- Forensic testimony should be limited to what is needed for successful prosecution. Utilization of charts, graphs, or other appropriate audiovisual aides showing forensic linkages will clearly and succinctly convey the facts of the cases.
- When necessary, investigators should seek independent, secondary reviews of laboratory results. This may be somewhat problematic, since there are crime laboratories that will not duplicate forensic examinations. sometimes made to this policy on a case-by-case basis.

Forensic evidence case vignette:

The case of serial child murderer Richard Mark Evonitz highlights the variety of forensic testing that may be utilized to solve difficult cases. In 1996 and 1997, in Spotsylvania County, Virginia, three young girls were abducted from their residences, sexually assaulted, and killed. The fi rst case occurred on September 9, 1996, when Sophia Silva disappeared from the front porch of her house. She was found in October of 1996, in a swamp, 16 miles from her residence. A suspect was arrested and charged for her murder, based on a faulty trace evidence examination conducted by a state laboratory.

On May 1, 1997, two sisters, Kristin and Kati Lisk, disappeared from their residence after returning home from school. Their bodies were discovered fi ve days later in a river, 40 miles from their residence. After an examination by an FBI Laboratory Examiner yielded trace evidence that positively linked the Silva and Lisk homicides to a common environment, the suspect arrested in the Silva case was subsequently released.

The investigation continued for an additional five years, until a girl was abducted in South Carolina. The victim was able to escape, and she identifi ed Richard Mark Evonitz as her attacker. Evonitz fl ed South Carolina and was sighted in Florida. After a high-speed chase with police, Evonitz committed suicide. The investigation revealed that Evonitz had lived in Spotsylvania, in 1996 and 1997.

Forensic searches were conducted on Evonitz's residence in South Carolina, his former residence in Spotsylvania, Virginia, and his car. A detailed trace examination of the evidence from these searches and the evidence obtained from the three victims revealed a number of hair and fi ber matches, providing suffi cient evidence to tie Evonitz to the three murders.

The following trace examinations linked Evonitz to all three homicide victims:

- Fibers from a bath mat.
- Fibers from an afghan.
- Fibers from two separate carpets in Evonitz's former home in Virginia.
- Carpet fi bers from the trunk of Evonitz's car.
- Head hair consistent with Evonitz.

A trace examination also linked fi bers from a pair of fur-lined handcuffs to the three homicide victims and the surviving victim.

The unique combination of different hair and fiber evidence yielded the "common environment" to which all of the victims and the offender were exposed.

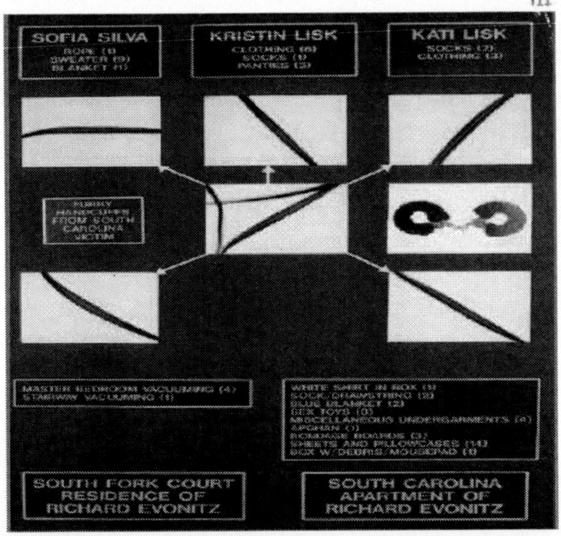

Latent fi ngerprints belonging to Kristin Lisk were located on the inside of the trunk lid of Evonitz's car, five years after the fact.

In: Serial Murderers
Editor: James T. Lawson, pp. 45-47
ISBN: 978-1-60692-204-0

Chapter 8

PROSECUTION OF SERIAL MURDER CASES

The recognition and investigation of a serial murder series is often perceived as a separate and distinct process from the other primary goal in these complex cases: the prosecution and conviction of the offender(s) responsible for the homicides. It was a consensus of Symposium attendees that law enforcement and prosecutors should work cooperatively as the investigative and prosecution processes are inextricably linked. When police suspect that one or more homicides may be the result of a serial killer, involving the prosecutor early on in the investigation may alleviate significant problems during trial.

The experience of the Symposium attendees was that in successful prosecutions of serial murder cases, the prosecutor's office was involved and remained accessible to law enforcement throughout the entire investigation and subsequent arrest. The partnership continued during the trial and resulted in the successful prosecution of the serial murderer.

The prosecutor can assist with critical decisions early in the investigation that could potentially impact on court admissibility. Maintaining the integrity of the legal process is a paramount consideration when dealing with court orders, search warrants, Grand Jury testimony, subpoenas, evidence custody matters, capital murder issues, and concerns related to the possible offender's competency and the voluntariness of confessions.

Prosecutors are also in the best position to evaluate the different murder cases within the serial investigation for presentation in court. They can provide important recommendations regarding the future use of evidence, forensic laboratory work, witness reports, and suspect interviews during trial.

Case management and investigative decision making are still controlled and managed by the law enforcement agencies. The prosecutor acts in an advisory capacity. The responsibilities and duties of the prosecutor should be clarified initially in the investigation to avoid potential confusion while the investigation progresses.

In multi-jurisdictional cases, variations in evidentiary standards, search warrant requirements, interview protocols, the quality of the evidence, and the ability to prosecute for capital murder may dictate the appropriate venue for prosecution. This consideration may take on greater significance when the crimes occur in different states.

Expert witnesses often play a significant role in high profile serial murder investigations, dealing with forensic and competency issues. In many investigations and prosecutions, the task of linking the defendant to the victim and the homicide scene(s) has been simplified because of physical, trace, and/or DNA evidence located at the scene. Expert forensic witnesses are utilized to explain the analysis and value of such evidence. Identifying and securing the services of forensic psychologists and psychiatrists will be important when addressing issues of competency, diminished capacity, and the insanity defense. Consideration should also be given for other collateral expert witnesses, who may be utilized to address issues outside of the customary topics, such as blood spatter.

Prosecution case vignette:

The Washington, D.C. Beltway sniper attacks serve as an excellent example of multi-jurisdictional prosecutorial considerations. The Beltway serial sniper attacks took place during three weeks of October 2002, in the Washington, D.C. metropolitan area. Ten people were killed and three others critically injured, in various locations throughout the metropolitan area. The killings actually began the month prior to the D.C. rampage, with these offenders committing a number of murders and robberies in several other states. The D.C. area shootings began on October 2nd, with a series of five, fatal shootings over a fi fteen-hour period in Montgomery County, Maryland, a suburban county north of Washington, D.C. The investigation was initially spearheaded from Montgomery County, and as the number of shootings mutiplied, the task force involved numerous local, state, and federal law enforcement agencies from Maryland, Virginia, and the District of Columbia. The two men responsible for the homicides, John Allen Muhammad and Lee Boyd Malvo, were eventually captured at an interstate rest area in Western Maryland.

It was ultimately decided that Fairfax County, Virginia, would have the first opportunity to try one of the murders, despite the fact that Maryland had more cases. It was felt that the case in Fairfax was the strongest case. The Fairfax

County homicide was the ninth in the Washington, D.C. area series and the third homicide in Virginia. A conviction for murder was secured in this case against Malvo, resulting in a life sentence.

Muhammad was tried next for Capital Murder in a case that occurred in Prince William County, Virginia, which resulted in a death sentence. Malvo, pursuant to a plea agreement, then plead guilty to one count of murder and one attempted murder in Spotsylvania County, Virginia, and was sentenced to life without parole.

Prosecutors in Montgomery County, Maryland, subsequently tried and convicted Muhammad on six counts of murder, and he was sentenced to six consecutive life sentences, without the possibility of parole. Malvo plead guilty and testified against Muhammad. During these trials, Malvo confessed to four other shootings in California, Florida, Texas, and Louisiana. It is unknown whether these or several other jurisdictions, including Arizona, Georgia, Alabama, and Washington State plan to prosecute Muhammad and Malvo.

In: Serial Murderers
Editor: James T. Lawson, pp. 49-52
ISBN: 978-1-60692-204-0

Chapter 9

MEDIA ISSUES IN SERIAL MURDER INVESTIGATIONS

Serial murder cases are inherently newsworthy. Some investigations last for years. Many attract attention because of the type of victims involved, and in others the serial killers themselves are media-attractive. Media attention is exacerbated by the insatiable demands of the twenty-four-hours-a-day, seven-days-a-week news reporting industry. The constant news attention on the investigation inevitably results in conflicts with law enforcement.

Often the relationship between law enforcement and the media is not a close one. In some law enforcement agencies, there is a long history of distrust and resentment underpinning this relationship. From the law enforcement perspective, the media publishes unauthorized information from investigations, hypothesizes on investigative progress, and uses talking heads to critique the investigative efforts. From the media's standpoint, law enforcement withholds too much information and does not communicate adequately with the media. It is counterproductive for law enforcement to sustain contentious relationships with the media, while attempting to develop an overall strategy for a successful serial murder investigation. The only party who benefits from this negative relationship is the serial murderer, who may continue to avoid detection. A respectful, cooperative relationship between law enforcement and the media will serve the missions of both.

It becomes essential for law enforcement personnel involved in a serial murder investigation to design and implement an effective media plan. The plan should provide timely information on a regular basis, without compromising the investigative endeavors. It is essential for media releases to be closely coordinated with investigative strategies. This helps determine the best times to both educate and solicit information from the public concerning certain aspects of the investigation. Once a media plan is established, law enforcement can be more proactive than reactive in its media strategy.

Symposium attendees provided a number of suggestions regarding media issues:

- Identify one spokesperson as the Public Information Officer (PIO), to speak on behalf of the investigation. This person would, in conjunction with other members of the investigative effort, prepare releases, make statements, and update the media on behalf of all involved jurisdictions, including forensic laboratories and medical examiners' offices. To eliminate confusion and controversy, MOUs should include an agreement regarding the designation of a single PIO in multi-jurisdictional, serial murder investigations.
- The role of the PIO is extremely demanding and time consuming, and they should not be assigned any additional investigative responsibilities. In addition, the PIO should have limited access to sensitive case facts. This will help minimize the possibility of critical information being inadvertently released to the media.
- The PIO must be aware that any verbal comments they make to augment information in the written press release can negate the strategy of the written press release. Any verbal comments made in conjunction with written press releases should be coordinated and rehearsed with the lead investigator(s), prior to the release.
- Press releases can be designed around several purposes: to announce a development in the case; to provide public safety information; to educate the public; to solicit information from the community; to provide behavioral information about the offender; to correct misinformation about the case; or to encourage someone who may know the offender to come forward.
- Press releases should always have very specific objectives. New releases should be reviewed by lead investigators and management, prior to dissemination. Investigators should consult with proven behavioral experts experienced in serial murder cases, before releasing any behavioral-based offender information.
- Press releases regarding the investigative effort should always have a positive tone. The PIO should continually remind the community that every available resource is being utilized in the investigation. A release can also include statements that discuss the impact of the case on the

community, including the nature and scope of the threat to potential victims and the steps being taken by law enforcement to educate the community.

- Inaccurate information distributed by the media regarding a serial murder investigation should be identified and addressed by law enforcement as soon as possible. Such information may include statements made by talking heads solicited by the media. This may require daily monitoring of news broadcasts and print media by investigators, to identify the incorrect statements or misinformation.
- Contact should be made as soon as possible with media outlets to have erroneous information corrected or retracted. If the media outlet will not address the issue, corrective press releases should be quickly disseminated, either verbally or in written form. Regular meetings with owners and managers of media outlets during the course of a serial murder investigation may help alleviate these issues.
- In high profile serial murder cases, the media may attempt to interact with members of the victims' families. Victims' families suffer emotionally from their loss and may interact with the media in ways that could negatively impact the case. A victim's family's goals and objectives may not correspond with those of law enforcement. This can be exacerbated when the investigation continues for a long period of time without conclusion. Establishing liaison with each of the victims' families is the simplest way to counteract this. As was discussed previously in the investigative section, a single law enforcement officer should act as a liaison for each of the victims' families. Aside from the traditional liaison role, the officer also educates the family as to the tenacious demands for information by the media and the potential negative consequences that unauthorized releases of information bring to the investigation.
- Law enforcement should be creative in considering non-traditional methods of disseminating information to the public. This is particularly important if the media is editing information disseminated by law enforcement. One suggestion is to create an investigation web page that is updated regularly and provides the public with unedited versions of press releases, regular updates on the status of the investigation, and other information designed to appropriately inform the public.
- Law enforcement should anticipate the inevitable public reaction resulting from an announcement that the investigation involves a serial killer. Either the media will link the cases and proclaim a serial murderer is operating, or investigators will proactively release the information. The

investigative team should be prepared for either situation. If the media makes the announcement, it is important for law enforcement to respond quickly, so they do not appear unprepared or defensive. If law enforcement plans on making the announcement, the release should be timed to gain an investigative advantage.

- There have been several serial killers who actively communicated with the police or the media. In these cases, investigators should consult with behavioral experts to assist with a proactive media strategy.

Media Strategy Case vignette:

The BTK case is an example of how a proactive media strategy contributed to the capture of a serial murderer. The BTK killer fi rst emerged in 1974 and, over time, killed a total of ten victims. From 1974 until 1988, BTK sent a series of five communications to the media, citizens, and the police in which he not only named himself BTK (Bind them, Torture them, and Kill them) but also claimed credit for killing a number of the victims. He abruptly stopped communicating in 1988. He re-emerged in 2004 by sending a new communication to the media. The Wichita Police Department formed a task force with the Kansas Bureau of Investigation, the FBI, and other agencies. The FBI's BAU-2 was contacted and provided a proactive media strategy that was utilized throughout the case. This strategy involved using the lieutenant in charge of the investigation to provide written press releases at critical times, which resulted in 15 press releases during the course of the investigation. BTK provided eleven communications to police and the media during the eleven-month investigation. The last communication BTK sent included a computer disk, containing information that eventually identified Dennis Rader as BTK. During Rader's interrogation, he commented positively on the press releases and his perceived relationship with the investigative lieutenant who issued the press statements.

In: Serial Murderers
Editor: James T. Lawson, pp. 53-55

ISBN: 978-1-60692-204-0

Chapter 10

ISSUES REGARDING TALKING HEADS IN THE MEDIA

The public's interest in serial murder cases makes serial murder an attractive storyline for the media. To further the public's interest in these cases, the media uses people who are willing to speak as experts on the topic of serial murder and more specifi cally, individuals willing to comment on the current, featured case. These commentators are commonly referred to as talking heads, and it appears that there is no shortage of people willing to do this.

Individuals utilized by the media to comment on serial murder cases include both experts and pseudoexperts. Experts are identified as academicians, researchers, retired law enforcement officials, mental health professionals, and retired law enforcement profilers who have developed specific knowledge and experience in serial murder investigations. Pseudoexperts are self-proclaimed profilers and others who profess to have an expertise in serial murder, when, in fact, their experience is limited or non-existent. The media will recruit talking heads, whether true experts or pseudoexperts, to offer their opinions on current cases, when they have no official role in the investigation and no access to any of the intimate facts of the case.

When individuals appear in the media and discuss ongoing cases, they have an enormous potential to negatively influence investigations and may even cause irreversible damage. They often speculate on the motive for the murders and the possible characteristics of the offender. Such statements can misinform the public and may heighten fears in a community. They may contribute to mistrust and a lack of confidence in law enforcement and, more importantly, may taint potential jury pools. These statements may also impact the behavior of the serial murderer, because it is unlikely that an offender discriminates between a talking head and a law enforcement official actively involved in the case. When offenders are challenged by statements or derogatory comments made in the media, they may destroy evidence, or more tragically, react violently.

Attendees of the Symposium were asked to discuss this issue and offer written comments. The following observations were made:

- Law enforcement is strongly encouraged to continue its release of information to the public during an investigation, in order to alert the community to a public safety issue or to solicit assistance in the identifi• information about an ongoing case and talking heads who comment on a case in which they have no investigative information. • Members of the media are encouraged to closely examine the credentials of any experts whom they are considering utilizing, to ascertain if the qualifiexperience level they claim is accurate. • fications listed on cation and/or capture of an offender. There is a difference between law enforcement agencies proactively releasing cations and When an expert is retained by the media, having the expert's qualia public website would offer the community the opportunity to assess the expert's authenticity and credibility.
- Responsible, retired law enforcement officers, clinicians, academicians, and researchers who are asked to provide statements concerning ongoing cases should refrain from doing so, unless requested by, or with the permission of, the agency who has jurisdictional responsibility over the case.
- Individuals who have developed an expertise in a given field recognize that before an opinion can be rendered, complete and accurate information must be obtained and analyzed. Therefore, it is inappropriate, even for acknowledged experts in serial murder, to offer opinions regarding a specific case based solely upon incomplete and potentially inaccurate information available through the media.

If responsible professionals are requested to provide statements about ongoing cases, the following guidelines are suggested:

- Speak in general terms only.
- Do not comment on the particulars of the current case.
- Do not criticize the investigative efforts.
- Do not misrepresent one's credentials or experience.

- Provide information to educate the public on the issues involved in serial murder.

It was the opinion of the experts at the Symposium that it is not possible to regulate or officially censor comments made by talking heads during serial murder investigations. However, a policy statement issued by law enforcement to the media would be appropriate, and below is an example of such a statement:

The media's role in reporting the facts of a case is a major public service. However, providing a forum for speculative commentary can be counter-productive and potentially dangerous. Public comments on an active investigation with incomplete or incorrect information are merely speculation and can seriously jeopardize an ongoing case and place citizens at great risk. Accordingly, we respectfully request that restraint be exercised and comments withheld until after an arrest has been made.

In: Serial Murderers
Editor: James T. Lawson, pp. 57
ISBN: 978-1-60692-204-0

EPILOGUE

We would once again like to recognize the individuals who attended and participated in the Serial Murder Symposium and thank them for their contributions. These individuals are among the world's most knowledgeable experts on serial murder. Many have been involved for years in the study of serial murder, and they have collectively published dozens of books and articles on a number of diverse topics related to serial murder. Their publications are recommended for anyone involved in investigating, prosecuting, or studying serial murder.

Due in a large part to the efforts of the professionals who attended the Symposium, there has been significant progress over the past few years in understanding serial killers and the crimes they commit. However, there is still much work to be done. Continued research in the topic areas addressed in this monograph is vital to advancing the knowledge on this important subject.

The men and women of the FBI's Behavioral Analysis Unit 2 look forward to continued partnerships in the collaborative efforts to better understand, and subsequently generate a more effective investigative response, to the serial killers that prey upon our citizens.

In: Serial Murderers
Editor: James T. Lawson, pp. 59-61
ISBN: 978-1-60692-204-0

APPENDIX A. SYMPOSIUM AGENDA

U.S. Department of Justice
Federal Bureau of Investigation

Serial Murder Symposium

San Antonio, Texas August 29 - September 2, 2005
Sponsored by the FBI's National Center for the Analysis of Violent Crime,
Behavioral Analysis Unit – 2, Crimes Against Adults

Monday, August 29, 2005

AGENDA

7:30 a.m. – 8:00 a.m.	**Continental Breakfast**
8:00 a.m. – 8:30 a.m.	**Welcome and Introductions** SSA Mark A. Hilts, Unit Chief, NCAVC, BAU-2 SSA Stephen E. Etter, Acting Assistant Special Agent in Charge NCAVC SA Robert J. Morton, NCAVC, BAU-2
8:30 a.m. – 9:15 a.m.	**Panel: Serial Murder Myths, Scope, Definitions, and Typologies** Speakers: SSA Robert J. Morton – Myths and urban legends Dr. Eric Hickey – Terms, definitions, typologies Dr. Tom Petee – Previous studies
9:15 a.m. – 10:15 a.m.	**Panel: Pathology/Causality** Moderator: Dr. Gregory Saathoff Speakers: Dr. Debra Niehoff – Biological/Neurological perspective Dr. Robert Hare – Psychopathy Dr. Jay Corzine – Criminological perspective Dr. Wade Myers – Developmental perspective
10:15 a.m. – 10:30 a.m.	**Morning Break**
10:30 a.m. – 11:45 a.m.	**Panel: Evaluation of Known Offenders** Moderator: SSA James J. McNamara Speakers: Judge Ann Keary Dr. Park Dietz Dr. Fred Berlin
11:45 a.m. – 1:00 p.m.	**Lunch on your own**
1:00 p.m. – 3:00 p.m.	**Case Presentation: Green River Killings** Moderator: SSA Mary Ellen O'Toole Det. Jon Mattsen Det. Tom Jensen Mr. Brian McDonald, Esq.
3:00 p.m. – 3:30 p.m.	**Afternoon Break**
3:30 p.m. – 5:30 p.m.	**Breakout Session #1**
5:30 p.m. – 5:45 p.m.	**Breakout Team Leader Meeting**

Tuesday, August 30, 2005

7:30 a.m. – 8:00 a.m.	**Continental Breakfast**
8:00 a.m. – 10:00 a.m.	**Panel: Media's Influence in Serial Murder Investigation** Moderator: SSA Mary Ellen O'Toole Speakers: Dr. Stephen Gorelick Ms. Mary Walsh Chief Pat Englade (retired) Dr. Eric Hickey
10:00 a.m. – 10:30 a.m.	**Morning Break**
10:30 a.m. – 11:45 a.m.	**Panel: Forensics in Serial Murder Cases** Moderator: SSA Armin A. Showalter Speakers: Dr. Tracey Corey Dr. John "Jack" Kenney Dr. Lee Goff Dr. William Rodriguez Dr. William Haglund SSA Douglas Deedrick (retired) UC Thomas F. Callaghan
11:45 a.m. – 1:00 p.m.	**Lunch on your own**
1:00 p.m. – 3:00 p.m.	**Case Presentation: Health Care Serial Murder** Moderator: MCS Timothy G. Keel Speakers: Dr. Brian Donnelly SAC Bruce Sackman VA OIG (retired)
3:00 p.m. – 3:30 p.m.	**Afternoon Break**
3:30 p.m. – 5:30 p.m.	**Breakout Session #2**
5:30 p.m. – 5:45 p.m.	**Breakout Team Leader Meeting**

Wednesday, 08/31/2005

7:30 a.m. – 8:00 a.m.	**Continental Breakfast**
8:00 a.m. – 8:30 a.m.	**Keynote Speaker – J. Stephen Tidwell** **Special Agent in Charge, Critical Incident Response Group**
8:30 a.m. – 10:00 a.m.	**Panel: Prosecution of Serial Murder Cases** Moderator: SSA Mark Safarik Ms. Barbara Corey Mr. Anthony Savage, Esq. Mr. Stephen Kay, Esq.
10:00 a.m. – 10:30 a.m.	**Morning Break**
10:30 a.m. – 11:45 a.m.	**Case Presentation: Ghana Serial Murder Case** Moderator: SSA Gerard F. Downes Speakers: Deputy Commissioner David Assante-Apeatu SSA Charles K. Dorsey
11:45 a.m. – 1:00 p.m.	**Lunch on your own**
1:00 p.m. – 3:00 p.m.	**Breakout Session #3**
3:00 p.m.	**Early Dismissal (Breakout team leaders briefly meet)**
5:00 p.m. – 8:30 p.m.	**Research Poster Session with Refreshments & Snacks**

Thursday, 09/01/2005

7:30 a.m. – 8:00 a.m.	**Continental Breakfast**	
8:00 a.m. – 10:00 a.m.	**Panel: Task Force and Major Case Management Issues**	
	Moderator:	MCS Kirk R. Mellecker
	Speakers:	Chief Cal Walker – Long term investigations
		Major Gary Terry – Problem recognition
		Mr. Lloyd Sigler – Major case management
		Mr. Ken Farnsworth - Multi-jurisdictional issues
		Mr. Jim Bell – Lead control issues
10:00 a.m. – 10:30 a.m.	**Morning Break**	
10:30 a.m. – 12:15 p.m.	**Case Presentation: Resendez Serial Murder**	
	Moderator:	SSA David T. Resch
	Speakers:	SSA Alan Brantley (retired)
		Mr. Charles Rosenthal, Esq.
		SA Mark Young (retired)
12:15 p.m. – 1:30 p.m.	**Lunch on your own**	
1:30 p.m. – 3:00 p.m.	**Case Presentation: Lewis Lent Serial Murder**	
	Moderator:	SSA Robert J. Morton
	Speakers:	SSA Gerard F. Downes
		Captain Frank Pace
		Sr. Investigator John Shultis
3:30 p.m. – 5:30 p.m.	**Breakout Session #4**	
5:30 p.m. – 5:45 p.m.	**Breakout Team Leader Meeting**	

Friday, 09/02/2005

7:30 a.m. – 8:00 a.m.	**Continental Breakfast**
8:00 a.m. – 9:00 a.m.	**Summary of Findings/Closing Remarks**
9:00 a.m.	**Checkout and Travel Home**

In: Serial Murderers
Editor: James T. Lawson, pp. 63-67
ISBN: 978-1-60692-204-0

APPENDIX B. SERIAL MURDER SYMPOSIUM WORKING GROUP SERIAL MURDER SYMPOSIUM WORKING GROUP

Dr. Kristen R. Beyer
Research Coordinator,
FBI CIRG, NCAVC

Alice E. Casey
Crime Analyst,
FBI CIRG, NCAVC

Dr. Maureen Christian
Professor of Psychology
Marymount University

Dr. Dewey Cornell
Professor
University of Virginia

Dr. Jay Corzine
Professor and Chair of
Sociology and Anthropology
University of Central Florida

Dr. Douglas Deedrick
Supervisory Special Agent (Retired), FBI

Forensic Science Division
Metropolitan Police Dept.
Washington, DC

Gerard F. Downes
Supervisory Special Agent,
FBI CIRG, NCAVC

Pamela J. Hairfield
Management and Program
Analyst, FBI
CIRG, NCAVC

Dr. Robert Hare
Professor of Psychology
Darkstone Research Group
University of British Columbia,
Canada

Dr. Eric Hickey
Professor, Dept. of Criminology
California State University,
Fresno

Mark A. Hilts
Unit Chief of BAU-2, FBI
CIRG, NCAVC

Dr. Earl James
Captain (Retired)
Michigan State Police
International Forensic
Services, Inc. Lansing,
MI

Dr. John Jarvis
Criminologist, FBI
Training and Development Division

Tom Jensen
Detective
King County Sheriff's Office
Kent, WA

Chris Johnson
Detective
Baton Rouge Police Department

Timothy G. Keel
Major Case Specialist, FBI
CIRG, NCAVC

Ken Landwehr
Lieutenant
Wichita Police Department

Dr. Wayne D. Lord
Unit Chief of BAU-3, FBI
CIRG, NCAVC

Steven F. Malkiewicz
Supervisory Special Agent, FBI
CIRG, NCAVC

James J. McNamara
Supervisory Special Agent, FBI
CIRG, NCAVC

Kirk R. Mellecker
Major Case Specialist, FBI
CIRG, NCAVC

Robert J. Morton
Supervisory Special Agent, FBI
CIRG, NCAVC

Dr. Wade Myers
Chief of Division and

Adolescent Psychiatry
University of South Florida

Dr. Mary Ellen O'Toole
Supervisory Special Agent, FBI
CIRG, NCAVC

David T. Resch
Supervisory Special Agent, FBI
CIRG, NCAVC

Dr. Gregory B. Saathoff
Associate Professor of Research
University of Virginia School of Medicine

Mark Safarik
Supervisory Special Agent, FBI
CIRG, NCAVC

Dr. Louis Schlesinger
Professor of Forensic Psychology
John Jay College of Criminal Justice

Armin A. Showalter
Supervisory Special Agent, FBI
CIRG, NCAVC

Melissa Smrz
Section Chief, FBI
Laboratory Division

Vito Spano
Chief Investigator
New York State Attorney
General's Office

Rhonda L. Trahern
Supervisory Special Agent, ATF
CIRG, NCAVC

Calvin Walker
Chief
Spokane Valley Police Department
Spokane Valley, WA

Dr. Michael Welner
Chairman
The Forensic Panel
New York, NY

Wilma B. Wulchak
Management and Program Analyst, FBI
CIRG, NCAVC

In: Serial Murderers
Editor: James T. Lawson, pp. 69-83
ISBN: 978-1-60692-204-0

Appendix C. Symposium Attendees

Symposium Attendees

Ewa-Marie Aghede
Detective Inspector
National Criminal Intelligence
Service Stockholm, Sweden

Larry G. Ankrom
Supervisory Special Agent
(Retired), FBI

David Asante-Apeatu
Deputy Commissioner
Ghana Police Service
Accra, Ghana

James O. Beasley, II
Supervisory Special Agent, FBI
CIRG, NCAVC

Jim Bell
Former Detective
Salt Lake City Police Department
Salt Lake City, Utah

Dr. Fred S. Berlin
Associate Professor

Department of Psychiatry and
Behavioral Sciences
Johns Hopkins University

Daniel G. Bermingham
Supervisory Special Agent, FBI
CIRG, NCAVC

Camille D. Bibles
Assistant United States
Attorney District of Arizona

Steven A. Bongardt
Supervisory Special Agent, FBI
CIRG, NCAVC

Alan C. Brantley
Supervisory Special Agent (Retired), FBI

John A. Brunell
Special Agent, FBI
Little Rock Field Office

Lesley A. Buckles
Crime Analyst, FBI
CIRG, NCAVC

Dr. Alexander Bukhanovskiy
Professor
Roston State Medical University
Roston-on-Don, Russia

Dr. Ann Burgess
Professor Boston College of Nursing

Alice E. Casey
Crime Analyst, FBI
CIRG, NCAVC

Dr. Maureen Christian
Professor of Psychology Marymount University

Dr. Peter I. Collins
Forensic Psychiatrist
Ontario Provincial Police
Orillia, Ontario, Canada

Mary B. Collins-Morton
Special Agent, FBI
Washington Field Office

Barbara Corey
Attorney at Law
Tacoma, WA

Dr. Tracey Corey
Chief Medical Examiner
Office of Chief Medical Examiner
Louisville, KY

Dr. Jay Corzine
Professor and Chair of Sociology
and Anthropology University of Central Florida

Mike Crooke
Chief
Cumberland Police Department
Cumberland, IN

Leslie D'Ambrosia
Special Agent Florida
Department of Law Enforcement

Keith Davidson
Inspector
Royal Canadian Mounted Police
Surrey, British Columbia, Canada

Dr. Harold Deadman
Supervisory Special Agent
(Retired), FBI

Dr. Douglas Deedrick
Supervisory Special Agent
(Retired), FBI
Forensic Science Division
Metropolitan Police Department
Washington, DC

Dr. Park Dietz
Park Dietz and Associates, Inc.
Newport Beach, CA

William H. Donaldson
Supervisory Special Agent, FBI
CIRG, NCAVC

Dr. Brian Donnelly
Special Agent, FBI
New Haven Field Office

Charles K. Dorsey
Supervisory Special Agent, FBI
CIRG, NCAVC

Gerard F. Downes
Supervisory Special Agent, FBI
CIRG, NCAVC

Dr. Steven A. Egger
Professor University of Houston at Clearlake

Pat Englade
Chief of Police
(Retired)
Baton Rouge Police Department

Stephen E. Etter
Unit Chief of BAU-1, FBI
CIRG, NCAVC

Kenneth Farnsworth
Chief Investigator Utah
Attorney General's Office

Dr. Adelle E. Forth
Professor of Psychology Carleton
University Ottawa, Ontario, Canada

Dr. James Alan Fox
Professor Northeastern University

Laurie R. Gibbs
Special Agent, FBI
Dallas Field Office

Dr. M. Lee Goff
Professor of Criminal Justice
Chaminade University of Honolulu

Paul Goodman
Investigator
Colorado Attorney General Office

Dr. Stephen Gorelick
Vice President for Institutional Advancement
The CUNY Graduate Center

Adam Gregory
Behavioral Investigative Advisor
National Crime and
Operations Facility
Bramshill Hook,
Hampshire, United Kingdom

Dr. William Haglund

Director International Forensic
Program Shoreline, WA

Pamela J. Hairfield
Management and Program Analyst, FBI
CIRG, NCAVC

Dr. Robert Hare
Professor of Psychology University
of British Columbia Darkstone Research
Group Vancouver, British Columbia, Canada

Robert R. (Roy) Hazelwood
Supervisory Special Agent (Retired), FBI

John J. Hess
Assistant Special Agent in Charge, FBI
CIRG, NCAVC

Dr. Eric Hickey
Professor Department of Criminology
California State University, Fresno

Mark A. Hilts
Unit Chief of BAU-2, FBI
CIRG, NCAVC

Tia A. Hoffer
Supervisory Special Agent, FBI
CIRG, NCAVC

Alexander Horn
Kriminalhauptkommissar
OFA Bayern
Munich City Police Department
Munich, Germany

Dr. Lin Huff-Corzine
Professor University of Central Florida

Kris Illingsworth
Detective Sergeant
New Wales Police Headquarters Parramatta,
New South Wales, Australia

Rick Jackson
Detective Los Angeles
Police Department

Dr. Earl James
Captain (Retired),
Michigan State Police International
Forensic Services, Inc. Lansing, MI

Dr. John P. Jarvis
Criminologist, FBI Training Division

Rick Jenkins
Captain, Division Commander
Virginia State Police Culpeper, VA

Tom Jensen
Detective King County Sheriff's Office Kent, WA

Leonard G. Johns
Supervisory Special Agent, FBI
CIRG, NCAVC

Chris Johnson
Detective
Baton Rouge Police Department

Stephen Kay
Deputy District
Attorney Los Angeles County District
Attorney's Office
The Honorable Ann Keary
Judge
Washington, DC Superior Court

Timothy G. Keel
Major Case Specialist, FBI
CIRG, NCAVC

Dr. John Kenney
Forensic Odontologist
DuPage County Coroner's Office
Park Ridge, IL

Robert H. Kosky, Jr.
Unit Chief of BAU-3, FBI
CIRG, NCAVC

Dr. Gretchen Witte Kraemer
Assistant Attorney General
State of Iowa

Dr. Gerard Labuschagne
Commander
South Africa Police Service
Pretoria, South Africa

Ken Landwehr
Lieutenant
Wichita Police Department

Jennifer A. Leonard
Supervisory Special Agent, FBI
FBIHQ, Washington, DC

Marianna Leshinskie
Interpreter, FBI
New York Field Office

Dr. Jack Levin
Professor of Criminal Justice
Northeastern University

Robert G. Lowery, Jr.

Commander
Greater St. Louis Major

Case Squad
Dr. Carl Malmquist
Professor
University of Minnesota

Colonel Rick Malone, M.D.
Chief of Forensic Psychiatry
Walter Reed Army Medical Center

R. Stephen Mardigian
Supervisory Special Agent
(Retired), FBI

John Martin
Sergeant
Texas Rangers San Antonio, Texas

Jon Mattsen
Detective
King County
Sheriff's Office Kent, WA

Brian M. McDonald
Deputy Prosecuting Attorney
King County Seattle, WA

James J. McNamara
Supervisory Special Agent,
FBI CIRG, NCAVC

Michael Medaris
Senior Policy Advisor
U.S. Department of Justice

Kirk R. Mellecker
Major Case Specialist, FBI CIRG, NCAVC

Dr. J. Reid Meloy
Associate Professor
Department of Psychiatry
University of California,
San Diego

Frank Merriman
Lieutenant (Retired)
Los Angeles Sheriff's Department,
Homicide Bureau

Thomas Monahan
Lieutenant
Las Vegas Metropolitan Police
Department

Paul Morrison
District Attorney
District Attorney's Office Olathe, KS

Robert J. Morton
Supervisory Special Agent, FBI
CIRG, NCAVC

Dr. Wade Myers
Chief of Division of Child and
Adolescent Psychiatry University of South Florida

Mike Napier
Supervisory Special Agent (Retired), FBI

Thomas M. Neer
Supervisory Special Agent, FBI
CIRG, NCAVC

Dr. Debra Niehoff
Neurobiologist Biotext Newtown, PA

Dr. Mary Ellen O'Toole

Supervisory Special Agent, FBI
CIRG, NCAVC Frank Pace Captain
New York State Police Loudonville, NY

John Perry
Special Agent Virginia State
Police Roanoke, VA

Dr. Tom Petee
Professor Auburn University

Pat Postiglione Sergeant
Nashville Metropolitan Police
Department

Patricia Prezioso
Assistant Attorney General
Division of Criminal Justice Trenton, NJ

Mark W. Prothero
Attorney at Law Hanis Greaney Law,
PLLC Kent, WA

Dr. John T. Rago
Professor of Law
Duquesne University

Lee Rainbow
Senior Behavioural Investigative
Advisor National Crime and
Operations Faculty
Bramshill Hook, Hampshire, United Kingdom

David T. Resch
Supervisory
Special Agent, FBI
CIRG, NCAVC

Dr. D. Kim Rossmo
Department of Criminal Justice Texas State University

Dr. Gregory B. Saathoff
Associate Professor of Research
University of Virginia, School of Medicine

Bruce Sachman
Special Agent in Charge (Retired), OIG
Veteran's Administration New York, NY

Mark Safarik
Supervisory Special Agent, FBI
CIRG, NCAVC

Dr. Gabreille Salfati
Professor
John Jay College of
Criminal Justice

Christina Schaub
Crime Analyst, FBI
CIRG, NCAVC

Carlo Schippers
Captain
Dutch National Police Agency
The Netherlands

Dr. Louis Schlesinger
Professor of Forensic Psychology
John Jay College of
Criminal Justice

Armin A. Showalter
Supervisory Special Agent, FBI
CIRG, NCAVC

John H. Shultis
Senior Investigator
New York State Police Latham, NY

Lloyd Sigler
Supervisory Special Agent (Retired), FBI

Howard Smith
Sheriff Spotsylvania County Sheriff's
Office Spotsylvania, VA

Melissa Smrz
Section Chief, FBI
Laboratory Division

Vito Spano
Chief Investigator
New York State Attorney
General's Office

Faye Springer
Senior Criminalist
Sacramento County Forensic
Services Laboratory

Jayne M. Stairs
Crime Analyst, FBI
CIRG, NCAVC

Suzanne D. Stiltner
Crime Analyst, FBI
CIRG, NCAVC

Dr. Michael Stone
Professor of Clinical Psychiatry
Columbia University

Dirk Tarpley
Special Agent, FBI

Kansas City Field Office

Ron Thill
Investigator San Diego
County District
Attorney's Office

Melissa L. Thomas
Supervisory Special Agent,
FBI CIRG, NCAVC

Roger Thomson
Sergeant Montgomery County Police
Department Rockville, MD

Rhonda L. Trahern
Supervisory Special Agent, ATF
CIRG, NCAVC

Ronald Tunkel
Supervisory Special Agent, ATF
CIRG, NCAVC

James Van Allen
Detective Sergeant
Ontario Provincial Police
Orillia, Ontario

Eva von Vogelsang
Detective Inspector
National Criminal Intelligence
Department
Stockholm, Sweden

Calvin Walker
Chief
Spokane Valley Police Department
Spokane Valley, WA

Mary E. Walsh
Producer
CBS News
Washington, DC

Dr. Michael Welner
Chairman
The Forensic Panel
New York, NY

Arthur E. Westveer, Jr.
Assistant Professor
Virginia Commonwealth University

Jeannine Willie
Assistant Manager
California Department of Justice
Missing Persons DNA Program
Sacramento, CA

Glenn Woods
Superintendent
Royal Canadian Mounted Police
Ottawa, Ontario Canada

Wilma B. Wulchak
Management and Program
Analyst, FBI
CIRG, NCAVC

Mark Young
Special Agent (Retired), FBI

INDEX

A

B

C

D

E

Q

R

S